LOW CARB

PROVEN LOW CARB HOMEMADE COOKBOOK THAT WILL HELP YOU LOSE WEIGHT WITHOUT STARVING

By

HANNAH PARKES

© 2016

Table of Contents

CHAPTER 1 5
LOW CARB DIETING; WHAT DOES IT MEAN? 5

Chapter 2 11
TYPICAL FOOD OF A LOW CARB DIET 11

Chapter 3. 16
LOW CARB DIET (THE REVIEW) 16

Chapter 4. 18
MEDICAL AND HEALTH BENEFITS OF LOW CARB DIETS 18

Chapter 5. 27
Mistakes associated with Low-Carb (Ways to Avoid Them) 27

Chapter 6. 32

THREE GENERAL APPROACHES TO LOW CARB DIETING: 32

Chapter 7. 35
SIX STEPS TO GIVE YOU A GREAT START 35

Chapter 8. 40
PROVEN LOW CARB HOMEMADE COOKBOOK THAT WILL HELP YOU LOSE WEIGHT WITHOUT STARVING 40

CHAPTER 1

LOW CARB DIETING; WHAT DOES IT MEAN?

INTRODUCTION

Low carb diet is a diet that seems to be changing the lives of people indulging it for the better. It has given people enough reasons for them to rethink the way they eat. In the early 70s, dietary guidelines were instituted around the globe in the early to promote the food pyramid which suggested that we reduce fats and consume a lot more carbohydrate. Carbohydrates were recognized as a very cheap and affordable source of energy (they still are). Reducing fats became the basis of health advice for the subsequent 40 years.

After a series of continuous research during these years, food researchers came to the conclusion that instead of reducing fats, we need to cut carbs. The increase in carbohydrate intake has contributed immensely to the pandemic of obesity and type 2 diabetes because carbohydrates act as stimulants for a hormone called insulin, which increases the body's glucose level. Carbohydrates are known to be the most efficient stimulator of insulin among the three most popular dietary macronutrients.

A low-carbohydrate diet is a term applied to foods that limit and reduce carbohydrate to less than the approved and recommended proportion or nothing less than 20% of caloric intake. Low carb diets are nutritional programs set up to help reduce, restrict and limit the intake of foods like pasta, sugar, bread, etc., that are very easy to digest and replace them with foods like meat, fish, egg, cheese, nuts, seeds, etc., that are very rich in fats and contain a higher level of adequate protein and other foods, mostly salad vegetables, known for their low carbohydrate content. Low carb diet help reduces the carbohydrates that are found in starchy vegetables, grains, and fruit to the minimum level while it highlights and lay emphasis on foods that have high protein content and fat. Low carb diets with a moderate amount of protein help you lose weight rapidly because they control and reduce cravings and make you feel satisfied for an extended period.

Every single diet has its guidelines, rules, and regulations that oversee and control the types of carbohydrates safe for your intake and the amounts of carbs you can eat. Restricting carbohydrate intake and consumption by engaging in low carb diets is not limited to its primary purpose of initiating effective weight loss only because some low-carb diets are known to have health benefits that go beyond weight loss. These low carb diets are used in the treatment, prevention and reduction of the risk factor of some long-lasting and chronic sicknesses and diseases like high blood pressure, diabetes, cardiovascular disease, auto-brewery syndrome, metabolic syndrome, etc.

Carbohydrates are a class of macronutrient that is present in many foods and drinks. They are mostly found naturally in plant-based foods like grains. Whenever they are in their natural state, they can either be considered to be complex and fibrous like the carbohydrates found in legumes and whole grains, or they can be seen as simple and less complex as well, like the carbohydrates that are present in milk and fruits in general. While carbohydrates that occur naturally are found in legumes, grains, fruits, vegetables, nuts, milk, seeds, and so on, refined carbohydrates also known as simple carbohydrates are produced artificially and are added in a sugary or floury form to processed foods during the process of food manufacturing. Examples of foods that fall into this category are cookies, candy, cake, pasta and white bread, sodas and drinks that have been sweetened with sugar.

The human body makes use of carbohydrates as its primary source of energy. During digestion, the consumed sugars and starches undergo a stage where they are all broken down into less complex carbohydrates, i.e. simple sugars. These simple sugars are afterward absorbed into your bloodstream where they become known as glucose (blood sugar). On the other hand, Fiber-laden carbohydrates don't get absorbed by your body as they tend to resist entirely, or substantially slow down the rate at which your digestive system processes digestion, even though they have a tiny effect on blood sugar. The increment in the level of blood sugar automatically initiates the release of insulin by your body. The primary purpose of insulin in the body is to build fat. Hence, if you're always eating Carbohydrates every three hours, you will end up having an increased insulin concentration in your blood consistently. The increased level of insulin concentration in your blood automatically drives the unabsorbed carbohydrates into the fat cells, thus making it impossible for the fat cells to release the fat. This sends a message to your brain that you are starving. The brain interprets this message accordingly and initiates the urge to go and eat in another 3 hours, which further releases insulin and increases the level of insulin concentration in your blood, accumulating a whole lot of fat in the process. The released insulin then paves the way for glucose to enter into your body's cells. Your body uses some of the glucose to fuel all its activities, and store excess glucose in your muscles, liver and other cells for future use or convert them to fat.

Despite the fact that dietary carbohydrates are usually the chief source of fuel in the body, they're not a vital macronutrient. If you remove, limit and reduce them from your diet, your body can switch to burning fat for energy instead. Lessening the level of carb intake by the body lowers the rate at which it releases insulin, causing it to convert stored fat into energy which eventually causes weight loss.

Chapter 2

TYPICAL FOOD OF A LOW CARB DIET

Generally speaking, a very extreme low-carb diet can be fairly limiting. This is because it excludes a lot of foods, mostly a lot of wholegrain foods. Even some fruits must be cut out as well. These are good and healthy foods that we are all very familiar with because we know they help in reducing the long-term risk of chronic disease. Many people consider wholegrain as a great source of energy and healthful food. It is always a tough thing to do when they are told to dispose those carbohydrates because they have started becoming more insulin resistant. Note that cutting the carbs in your diet does not imply that you should completely get rid of wholegrain in your diet; this only indicates that it is important to reduce the amount of wholegrain in your diet to a moderate level if you are among the most susceptible fraction of the populace that can't put up with them.

Low Carb diets are also beneficial to an athlete. It has always been presumed that carbs are an indispensable fuel source for you if you are the type that engages in exercise a lot. Recent researches, however, shows that eating a lot of carbohydrates only help whenever you are in need of a quick source of fuel for your body. Endurance athletes on low carbs can last just as long by burning fat for fuel. For an event that is going to last for two to three hours, carbohydrates simply don't have any advantage. The more little carbs you eat in your diet, the more adapted you become as an athlete. You can burn a huge amount of fat if you're a top athlete and simply cover a very good performance running very fast by taking low carbs. This is made possible by the action of Ketones. Ketones replace the majority of the human body's requirement for glucose. They serve as the substitute for the fuel source. They're created during the process of burning fat and converting it into energy, and can be measured in the blood or urine.

A low-carb diet mainly consists of foods that are rich in protein like fish, meat, eggs, poultry, and some vegetables that are non-starchy. Foods like bread, pasta, legumes, fruits, nuts and seeds and starchy vegetables are mostly excluded or limited in a low carb diet. A few number of low-carb diet plans, however, permit the intake of some fruits, grains and vegetables on a minimal level. A low-carb diet should be limited to around 60-130 grams per day. This level of carbohydrate intake produces 240-520 calories. Quite some low-carb diets substantially limit their daily carbohydrates intake to 60 grams or less during the initial stage of the diet and then continually increase the number of permitted carbs. The continuous occurrence of type 2 diabetes and obesity implies that new dietary methods are needed to conquer the epidemic. Food researchers have recommended some level of carbohydrate restriction as the ideal choice for a new dietary approach, and we present an all round review regarding carbohydrate restriction.

The analysis of foods and nutrition that were in place before modernization can remind everybody of the important capability of humans to get used to their surroundings and can arrange for a platform within which to view present-day diets. In contrast to present-day Western diets, the diets of many people before the advent of agriculture were quite low in carbohydrate. For instance, the local diets of many Aboriginal Canadians in North America before European migration consist of fish, meat, berries and wild plants. Not until the late 1800s when several North American aboriginal populations started changing their lifestyle and diets that the several health issues were widely known. Even though many aspects of their way of life were changed and transformed with civilization, these analysts suspected that the health problems originated from the change in diets, precisely from the introduction of sugar and flour. Similarly, before the discovery of insulin, removing high-glycemic carbohydrates like flour and sugar from the foods of diabetics was discovered to be an efficient and a successful way of regulating glycosuria (a condition where the amounts of glucose excreted in urine are higher than normal). While analyzing the pattern of food intake during the more recent obesity and diabetes epidemic, it was discovered that the surge in the number of calories present in the body was almost completely due to an increase in carbohydrate intake.

Going by this analysis, it is reasonable to suggest that diets that are very low in carbohydrate might be as healthy as, or even more vigorous than, the diets with higher carbohydrate content introduced into modern society only of late. This thematic review sums up all the studies that comprise of low-carbohydrate diets (LCDs)

Chapter 3.

LOW CARB DIET (THE REVIEW)

Over the past 50 years, our dietary consumption has considerably increased in correspondence with the epidemics of obesity, diabetes, and malnutrition. Food researchers, scientists, and physicians have been corroborating the health hazards linked to excess carbohydrates intake. Scientific researches and experiments have established the advantages of limiting carbohydrates intake. These benefits include weight loss as well as reduced diabetes and heart disease indicators. Even though some individuals are going to do as well or even better with a low-fat diet, a majority of the people will lose weight while on a low-carb diet. Therefore, going on a low carb diet is not the only the most efficient way to lose weight, but it has also been discovered to be the most widely successful diet plan that helps lose weight without starving. For nearly everybody, a low-carbohydrate diet is more satisfying, bearable, workable and active in its nutrient density.

Low-carb diets have been debated upon widely for years. They were initially criticized and strongly condemned by fat-phobic health practitioners and the media. People assumed that low carb diets would increase the body's cholesterol level and cause heart disease because of the high fat content. This is a misconception of the idea behind low carb diets that were nurtured by many people back then but has now been disapproved.

Ever since the year 2002, more than 20 human studies have been carried out on low carb diets. In nearly every one of those studies, it was discovered that low carb diets come out ahead of the other diets being compared to. Low carb diets do not only show better weight loss but also causes significant improvements in risk factors to occur, and includes cholesterol.

CHAPTER 4.

MEDICAL AND HEALTH BENEFITS OF LOW CARB DIETS.

1. Low Carb Diets Kill Your Appetite (in a Good Way).

The single most awful side effect of dieting is hunger. It is known to be one of the key reasons why many people feel dejected and depressed and finally give up on their diets. One of the best things about eating low-carb is that it helps to reduce craving and leads to an automatic reduction in appetite. The studies regularly indicate that whenever people eat low carbs by taking more protein and fat, they end up eating much fewer calories. When comparing low carb diets to low fat diets in the studies, researchers actively limit and restrict calories in the low-fat groups to ensure uniformity and make the results. When food researchers are comparing low-carb and low-fat diets in studies, they need to restrict calories actively in the low-fat groups to make the results equivalent. This shows that whenever people eat low carbs, their appetites have a tendency to reduce and go down, and they frequently end up taking a much smaller amount of calories without trying.

2. Low Carb Diets Lead to More Weight Loss

Eating low carbs is one of the modest and most efficient ways to lose weight. Studies show that people on low carb diets lose more weight, more rapidly than people on a low-fat diet without regarding the fact that the low-fat dieters are actively limiting their calorie level. The primary reason why this happens is that low carb diets help get rid of excess water from the body. The kidney contributes to reducing the level of insulin content in the body by shedding excess sodium which eventually leads to massive weight loss within the first three weeks. While making a comparison between low-carb diets and low-fat diets, the low-carb diet groups tend to lose 2 to 3 times as much weight without getting hungry.

Low-carb diets seem to be mainly useful for up to 6 months, after which the weight start to come back because people stop taking low carb diets and go back to their old eating habits. A low carb diet can be considered as being more of a lifestyle than a diet. The only way to get the best out of it is to stick to it without deviating. Low carb diets are without any doubts the most effective diet plan for losing weight, particularly in the first six months compared to other diet plans.

3. Body fat is not completely the same as they tend to vary a little.

The location of the fat in the body controls the way it will affect our health and risk of disease. Predominantly, the human body consist of two primary type of fat, subcutaneous fat (refers to fat that are located under the skin) and visceral fat (refers to fat that are found and stored in the abdominal cavity).Visceral fat is found around the body organs. The presence of a lot of fat in that area can bring about inflammation and resistance to insulin. This is alleged to be the main reason behind the metabolic dysfunction that is so prevalent in Western countries and some other parts of the world.

Low carb diets have been proven to be a very effective way of reducing the accumulated fat present in the abdominal cavity. Apart from being a very effective way to reduce fat and shed weight quickly and rapidly, low carb diets ensure that a great proportion of the fat being cut comes from the abdominal cavity. After a while, it should lead to a significantly reduced risk of type 2 diabetes and heart disease. Summarily, it can be deduced from the studies that a significant fraction of the lost fat on low carb diets appears to come from the harmful fat located in the abdominal cavity that is well-known to cause severe metabolic dysfunctions.

4. Triglycerides have a tendency to go way down with low carbs.

Low carb diets have been proven from the studies to be a very effective means of lowering blood triglycerides, which are fat molecules present in the blood and a well-known risk factor for heart-related diseases. Reduction in the level of carbohydrates intake tends to have a very vivid decrease in the level of triglycerides present in the blood.

5. Increased Levels of HDL

Low carb diets comprise of foods that have a high level of fat content, leading to a remarkable increase in blood levels of High Density Lipoprotein, otherwise known as the good cholesterol. This name comes as a result of its ability to lower the risk factor of heart-related diseases. HDL levels increase rapidly on low carb diets while they tend to show little or no increment or even go decrease on low-fat diets. This is because of the high level of fat content present in low carb diets which are known to be one of the best ways to increase HDL levels in the body. The ability to lower the amount of triglycerides in the blood and raise HDL levels makes low-carb diets the perfect diet plan for weight loss.

6. Reduced Blood Sugar and Insulin Levels, With a Major Improvement in type 2 Diabetes.

Reducing the intake of carbohydrate is one of the most efficient ways to lower blood sugar and insulin levels. This is also used in the treatment and possibly the reversal of type 2 diabetes.

7. Blood Pressure tends to go down

Having a high blood pressure otherwise known as hypertension is one of the most important risk factors for many diseases like heart disease, kidney failure, stroke and many others. Studies show low-carb diets to be an effective way of reducing blood pressure, which eventually help to reduce the risk of these diseases and help you live longer in life.

8. Low-Carb Diets Are The Most Effective Treatment Known Against Metabolic Syndrome.

Low-carb diets are very effective in reversing the five major signs of the metabolic syndrome, a severe health condition known to predispose people to type 2 diabetes and heart disease. Metabolic syndrome can be simply defined as a medical condition highly related to the risk of diabetes and heart disease. It is a list of symptoms of abdominal obesity, high blood pressure, high blood sugar levels, high triglycerides level and low HDL levels. Low carb diet, however, helps to tackle these symptoms and reduce their risk factors significantly.

9. Low Carb Diets help improve the Pattern of LDL Cholesterol.

Eating a low carb diet changes your LDL pattern change from small (bad) LDL to large LDL, which is non-threatening. Eating low carb diets also help in reducing the number of LDL particles moving around in the bloodstream. Studies show that people with high level of LDL are much more likely to have heart attacks. On the other hand, scientists have discovered that knowing the type of LDL is crucial in this situation because all of them are not of the same size. This makes the size of the particles very important. People with predominantly small particles are likely to have heart disease, whereas people who have mostly large particles are not. Low carb diets turn particles of LDL from small particles to large particles while helping to reduce the amount of LDL particles present in the bloodstream.

10. Low Carb Diets assist in the treatment of several brain disorders

Chapter 5.

Mistakes associated with Low-Carb (Ways to Avoid Them)

According to researchers, there are various issues that are likely to confront people that are eating low carb diets which can bring about an adverse effect, undesired and unpleasant results. Getting the best out of low carb diets and enjoying all the metabolic advantages of low-carb diets require more than just cutting back on the level of carbohydrates intake. It is possible you were making some common mistakes if after you have started eating low carb diets; you have not gotten the expected results. Listed below are some errors that prevent people from getting the best results from low carb

1. Eating Too Many Carbs.

What constitutes a proper low carb diet is not clearly defined. If you are planning to go fully into ketosis and enjoy all the metabolic advantages of a low carb diet, taking less than 50 grams of carbs per day may be essential. This will help flood your bloodstream with ketones and act as an efficient source of energy to your brain. However, this could be very limiting as it only leaves you with a few carb options like vegetables and small amounts of berries.

2. Eating Too Much Protein.

Protein is an essential macronutrient, needed in abundance by almost everybody. It can improve satiety and helps increase the rate at which the human body burns fat. Usually, taking too much protein ought to initiate weight loss and enhanced body composition. Low carb dieters eating a lot of protein in the form of animal foods may end up eating too much of them. Taking too much protein than your body needs leads to a process whereby your body converts the amino acids in protein to glucose through a process known as gluconeogenesis. This will eventually stop your body from going into complete ketosis which can later turn out to be a problem on most ketogenic and very low carb diets.

3. Being Afraid of Eating Fat.

Many people derive the most of their calories from dietary carbohydrates like grains and sugars. Removing this energy source from your diet requires finding a new source of energy to avoid starvation and malnourishment. Regrettably, some people believe that low fat in combination with a low carb will even be better since low carb is good enough on its own. This is not right as it has not been scientifically proven to be a good idea. You should ensure that your low carb diets contain very high fat content so as to get enough energy to sustain yourself.

4. Not Replenishing Sodium

Reduction in the level of insulin in the human body is one of the primary mechanisms behind low-carb diets. Insulin helps the body store fat and makes it possible for the kidneys to be able to retain sodium during excretion. Low-carb diets reduce the level of insulin in the body making the kidneys shed a significant amount of sodium from the body during excretion. This will eventually lead to a minor sodium deficiency in the body which causes fatigue, lightheadedness, constipation and headaches. You can prevent this by adding more sodium into your diet. Try as much as possible to take a cup of broth per day and add enough salt to your foods as they are both known to be an excellent source of Sodium.

5. Not Being Patient

The human body is built to burn carbs and correctly converts them to energy if available. Cutting back on carbohydrates means your body needs to source for energy elsewhere, which comes either from your accumulated fat stored in your body or from your diet. Since your body is used to burning carbs for energy, it will take a few days or many weeks (for full adaptation) for your body to get used to burning fat for energy. You should adhere strictly to your diet and be patient during the early stage so that the metabolic adaptation can occur.

The healthy carbohydrate recommendations for the general public state that about 50 to 65% calorie content in a diet ought to be from carbohydrate, consequently anything less than the recommended value is often referred to as low carb.

Chapter 6.

THREE GENERAL APPROACHES TO LOW CARB DIETING:

1. Just reduce carbohydrate-

This method is especially focused on limiting and completely removing added sugars, processed foods, and other refined carbohydrates. This reduction is beneficial because many of us have exceeded the recommended amount of carbohydrates for our body. Removing all kinds of sugary foods like white rice, white flour and potatoes from your diet, known as The White Foods is a typical example of this approach.

2. Find the best amount of carbohydrate for each person-

There is a level to which an individual can tolerate carbohydrate, and it differs from the way another person can tolerate carbohydrate. As you continue to grow older, your carbohydrate tolerance rate decreases, and your glucose becomes more responsive to carbohydrate regardless of whether your blood glucose level is normal or not. You also tend to develop resistance to insulin, probably because the pancreas cells responsible for the production of insulin have been damaged. Approaches that try to find the best carbohydrate level often recommend decreasing carbohydrate to a relatively low level and then start adding carbohydrate bit by bit until it gets to point when you discover that your weight loss ceases, weight gain occurs, you start craving for carbs again, your blood glucose control diminishes and your blood triglycerides rise. You would then have to reduce your carbohydrate intake from that point. The Atkins and South Beach diets are some of the examples of this approach.

3. Follow a ketogenic dietary plan (Keto-adaptation) -

A ketogenic diet is a form of food in which the body uses fat for its primary source of energy in the place of glucose. Putting your body in a keto-adaptation or fat adaptation state provides you with some metabolic benefits like improved stamina, endurance, etc. The body rarely runs out of fuel either between meals or during exercise because of the relative availability of fat in the body. This type of plan is used in the treatment of epilepsy, and there are ongoing researches to discover ways of treating different disorders through this kind of diet. While there is some individual dissimilarity, taking foods with moderate protein content and less than 60g of carbohydrate daily is ketogenic for many people while a few others have the ability to take as much carbohydrate as 100g in a single day and remain in ketosis.

Chapter 7.

SIX STEPS TO GIVE YOU A GREAT START

Do you intend to go on a low carb? Here are some tips you need to know before you start:

So you've made up your mind to reduce the level of your carb intake. Now, what is next?

1. Be Informed.

Research and read books that are based on different low carb diets or set your focus on one that is good for your body system. Preferably, read one of the books and get used to the principles of low carbs. Never fall for the common fables going round about low carb. Just like any other dietary plan, low carb eating may be balanced or not balanced, hygienic or not clean, healthy or not healthy, and it doesn't have any reason to be boring. With the aid of research, it has been proven times without number that cutting carbs are an efficient method of losing weight and help reduce the risk factors of some life threatening diseases in most people.

2. Start Making Easy Changes.

You can begin cutting out some unhealthy carbohydrates in your diet while you continue learning about low carb dieting. Decide on one or two things to change in your diet at a time. You will discover that putting in just a little effort will help you reach your targets quicker than you thought.

3. Decide on an Approach.

Although all of the approaches cut out a significant amount of sugar and some starches from their food choices, you still have to be specific with which approach you want to follow and stick to it. You can read books that are relevant to low carb or research it online and go for an approach that seems doable to you. On the other hand, if you are the type that doesn't like following someone else's idea of a diet, you might want to consider following the "No White Diet" as it seems to work for almost everybody. All you have to do is just to stop taking diets that contain white flour, i.e., bread, cake, donuts, pasta, etc., sugars, white rice, and potatoes. This efficiently reduces the level of carbohydrate content in your food. However, there are some white foods that have low carbohydrate content that's right for you. Examples are cauliflower, tofu, and onions.

4. Get Familiar with What You Can Eat.

Thinking about what you can't eat is quite easy when you are on a low carb, but it takes real productivity to focus on what you can eat. As a starter, it's best to follow a simple routine. You could keep making the same dinner as before, the only thing you have to replace (with starch) is the vegetables.

5. Plan Your First Week

There is nothing as discouraging as getting to the fifth day and you discover that you have nothing to eat. Early planning of your menus and snacks for a week saves you all the worries because you will always have something to eat, even in an emergency.

6. Get Support

Certainly; you will come across challenges, and things you didn't even think of will happen. Seek advice from others who are well experienced about low carb. You must be ready to work through these unforeseen circumstances and not be deterred by them.

Chapter 8.

PROVEN LOW CARB HOMEMADE COOKBOOK THAT WILL HELP YOU LOSE WEIGHT WITHOUT STARVING

Planning what diets you should take hang on a few things, and these include how healthy you are, the weight you are to lose and how often you exercise.

The Basics of a low carb diet meal

Your diet should be centered on these real, natural, low carb foods. The foods include:

Meat;

Beef meat, pork meat, lamb meat, chicken, turkey, and others should be on top of your diet list. Under this category, grass-fed beef is the most preferred.

Fish;

Salmon, trout, haddock and many others should also be a major constituent of your diet. Under this category, wild-caught fish is the best.

Eggs;

Pastured eggs are preferred.

Vegetables;

Vegetables like spinach, carrot, broccoli, cauliflower are recommended.

Fruits

like oranges, apples, pears, blueberries, and strawberries should regularly be taken

Nuts and Seeds;

Walnuts, almonds, sunflower seeds are good examples of nuts and shields that you should take when you are on a low carb.

High-Fat Dairy;

People whose diet constitute a lot of high-fat dairies like butter, cheese, heavy cream and yogurt rarely suffer from obesity and diabetes pandemic.

Fats and Oils;

Lard, butter, coconut oil, olive oil and cod fish liver oil should also be included in your low carb diet list. If you are very active, healthy and lean, you can add some tubers like potatoes and sweet potatoes, as well as some grains that are good for your health like rice and oats. Ice cream, candy, agave, fruit juices and other soft drinks that are very rich in sugar content should be avoided. Other foods you should avoid include gluten grains like spelt, barley, wheat, rye, pasta and bread, trans fats, seeds, artificial sweeteners like saccharin, sucralose, etc.

Foods that have very low-fat content like dairy foods, cereals, etc., and highly processed foods should all be removed from your diet list.

Low Carb Food List – Foods to Eat

If you are taking low carb diets to lose weight, you should be cautious with the way you eat cheese and nuts because you might get quickly addicted to eating them in a more-than-recommended proportion. You should also try to reduce the number of fruits you take in a day.

A Sample Low-Carb Menu for One Week

This is a typical illustration of a low carb diet plan for a week. It constitutes less than 50 grams of total carbs per day, but as stated earlier, you can go further than that if you are healthy, active and you don't need to lose weight.

DAY 1- Monday

Breakfast: Omelet with some vegetables, deep-fried in butter or coconut oil.

Lunch: Grass-fed yogurt, blueberries, and a few almonds.

Dinner: Cheeseburger with vegetables and salsa sauce.

DAY 2- Tuesday

Breakfast: Bacon and eggs.

Lunch: Remaining burgers and vegetables from the previous night.

Dinner: Salmon with vegetables and butter.

DAY 3- Wednesday

Breakfast: Eggs and vegetables, deep fried in butter or coconut oil.

Lunch: Shrimp salad together with olive oil.

Dinner: Meshed chicken with vegetables.

DAY 4- Thursday

Breakfast: Omelet with different vegetables, deep fried in coconut oil or butter.

Lunch: Smoothie mixed with coconut milk, almonds, protein powder, and berries.

Dinner: Vegetables and steaks.

DAY 5- Friday

Breakfast: Bacon and Eggs.

Lunch: Chicken salad together with some olive oil.

Dinner: Pork chops with vegetables.

DAY 6- Saturday

Breakfast: Omelet with different vegetables.

Lunch: Grass-fed yogurt together with berries, walnuts and coconut flakes.

Dinner: Meatballs with vegetables.

DAY 7- Sunday

Breakfast: Bacon and Eggs.

Lunch: Smoothie with coconut milk, a bit of heavy cream, chocolate-flavored protein powder, and berries.

Dinner: Grilled chicken wings with some raw spinach on the side.

Ensure that your diet consists of abundant low carb vegetables. If you are aiming to continue under 50 grams of carbs per day, then you can probably add more vegetables to your diet and take at least one fruit per day.

Examples of Healthy, Low Carb Snacks

Eating more than three times in a day doesn't have any particular health backing, but listed below are some easy to prepare, good low carb snacks that you can take to satisfy yourself whenever you get hungry before meal time.

i) Two baby carrots from the previous night or a hard-boiled egg

ii) You can take some cheese with meat too just before the next meal.

iii) Full fat yogurt or some few nuts

iv) A single piece of Fruit

Eating at Restaurants

Making your meal low carb friendly whenever you go out to eat in a restaurant is quite straightforward and very simple. All you have to do is to make a request for a fish or meat-based main dish and ask them to deep-fry your meal in real butter. Then you should get more vegetables to replace rice, bread or potatoes.

A Simple Low-Carb Shopping List

Shopping at the perimeter of the store where it is more likely to find all the foods in one piece is advisable. Grass-fed foods are preferable if you can afford them. If not, try to select the less processed foods that fall within your budget. Your shopping list should consist of foods like:

- i) Meat (chicken, bacon, beef, lamb, and pork),
- ii) Fish rich in fat like Salmon is preferable.
- iii) Omega-3 enriched eggs are preferable to conventional eggs.
- iv) Frozen vegetables like carrots and broccoli.

Some Healthy Low-Carb Meals in Under 40 Minutes

Here are some weight-loss friendly and easy to prepare low carb diets.

All Purpose Low Carb Baking Mix

Estimated preparation time- five minutes

Net carbohydrate content (in grams) - 4.9g

Protein content (in grams) – 31.3g

Fat content (in grams) – 4.4g

Fiber content (in grams) – 3.2g

Calories- 191cal

Ingredients:

i) crude wheat bran (1/4 cup)
ii) ii) whole grain soy flour
iii) iii) vanilla whey protein (2/3 cup)
iv) wheat gluten flour (2/3 cup)

Guidelines:

Add all ingredients together and mix thoroughly for 3-4 minutes. This should be taken immediately after preparation. It can also be stored in a sealed container for a month. Every single recipe makes 3 cups which can be served for up to 9 times. The serving size is 1/3 cup.

Coconut Muffin and Almond

Estimated Preparation time- 3 minutes

Net carbohydrate content (in grams) – 3.5g

Protein content (in grams) – 9.7g

Fat content (in grams) – 16.8g

Fiber content (in grams) –3g

Calories- 207cal

Ingredients:
i) almond meal flour (1/8 cup)
ii) 1/3 tablespoon of organic high fiber coconut flour
iii) 1 teaspoon of sucralose-based sweetener
iv) 1/2 teaspoon of cinnamon
v) baking powder (1/4 teaspoon)
vi) one large egg (omega-3 pastured egg is preferable
vii) 1/8 teaspoon salt
viii) 1/3 tablespoon of extra virgin olive oil

Guidelines:

Put all dry ingredients in a cup and begin stirring to combine the dry ingredients. Then add egg and oil, and then mix thoroughly.

Cook inside a microwave for a minute. Remove the entire muffin completely from the cup and eat.

Almond Protein Pancakes

Estimated Preparation time- 5 minutes

Net carbohydrate content (in grams) – 4.4g

Protein content (in grams) –20g

Fat content (in grams) – 9.9g

Fiber content (in grams) – 1.6g

Calories- 191cal

Ingredients:

i) Two vanilla flavored whey protein
ii) ii) Almond meal flour (1/4 cup)

iii) Three tablespoons of whole grain soy flour
iv) iv) One teaspoon of baking powder
v) Three big eggs
vi) Creamed cottage cheese (1/3 cup)

Guidelines:

Serve with almond butter or sugar-free pancake syrup. Garnish with toasted almonds, if desired. Add all the ingredients together and mix thoroughly. Combine the three eggs and blend the mixed eggs with the creamed cottage cheese.

Pour inside a griddle and heat it up, then add about 1/4 cup per pancake and turn over as soon as bubble starts forming, then wait for about two minutes until it is firm. You can serve with almond or any other non-sugary pancake syrup.

Beef Huevos Rancheros on Canadian Bacon

Estimated Preparation time- 20 minutes

Net carbohydrate content (in grams) – 2.5G

Protein content (in grams) – 23.1G

Fat content (in grams) –15g

Fiber content (in grams) – 0.6g

Calories- 244cal

Ingredients

i) Six ounces of ground beef
ii) Canned green chili peppers (1/2 cup)
iii) 1/4 teaspoon of garlic powder
iv) One teaspoon of chili powder
v) 1/4 teaspoon of cumin
vi) 1/4 teaspoon leaf oregano
vii) 1/4 teaspoon of salt
viii) 1/4 teaspoon of black pepper
ix) Four slices of Canadian bacon
x) Four large eggs
xi) 1/2 cup of shredded cheddar cheese
xii) 4 sprigs cilantro

Guidelines:

In a greased griddle, heat the beef up. Add garlic powder, chili powder, cumin, salt, oregano, and pepper, stir thoroughly then cook for about 10 minutes to blend the flavors. Position the Canadian bacon on top of the mixed beef and apply heat. Remove the griddle from the heat source and put it in a separate place. Mix the eggs in another grill and apply heat until they solidify. Put a slice of Canadian bacon on every single plate and add 1/4 beef mixture and 1/4 of the scrambled eggs. Add a little quantity of cheese and chopped cilantro.

Basque Eggs with Ham, Tomatoes and Bell Peppers

Estimated Preparation time- 30 minutes

Net carbohydrate content (in grams) – 6.9g

Protein content (in grams) – 19.6g

Fat content (in grams) – 30.2g

Fiber content (in grams) – 1.1g

Calories- 379cal

Ingredients:

i) Three tablespoons of extra virgin olive oil

ii) One medium-sized onions

iii) Eight ounces of roasted bell peppers

v) Two red tomatoes
vi) Five 1/2 tablespoons basil
vii) vi) 1/4 teaspoon red or cayenne pepper
viii) Twelve large eggs
ix) Six tablespoons of unsalted butter stick
x) Six ounces of boneless, cooked fresh ham
xi) x) Three teaspoons of garlic

Guidelines

Pour oil on a large griddle and heat it up slightly. Brown the onion for five minutes until it becomes soft; you can then add garlic and cook for another one minute. Add tomatoes, cayenne, and roasted peppers, then cook for ten minutes, staring intermittently, so that the vegetables will become soft. Open the griddle and apply medium heat till the sauce gets thick. Add seasonings like salt and pepper to give a great taste and good flavor. Blend the twelve eggs in a big bowl. Add the blended eggs and basil in a griddle together with the already softened butter and cook for 12 minutes, repeatedly stirring with a rubber spatula. Then add ham and pepper mixture and stir continuously.

Cheeseburgers without the Bun

Ingredients:

    i) Butter

    ii) Hamburgers,

    iii) Cheddar cheese

    iv) Cream cheese

    v) Salsa

    vi) Spices

    vii) Spinach

Guidelines:

Add butter into a skillet and heat it up until it melts, and then add spices and burgers. Flip till it's almost ready, and then add a few slices of cheddar cheese on top of it. Reduce the heat and cover up the skillet until the cheese melts. You can then choose to add some Salsa on top of the burgers to make it delicious.

Cheese-Filled Chicken Breast

Estimated Preparation time- 20m

Ingredients :

    i) Two tablespoons of olive oil

    ii) One garlic clove

    iii) One bell pepper

    iv) Four chicken breasts

    v) Two tablespoons pickled japalenos

    vi) 1/2 teaspoon of finely chopped cumin salt and pepper

    vii) Four toothpicks

    viii) One cup of shredded cheese (240ml)

    ix) Three ounces of cream cheese (90g)

Guidelines:

Heat up your oven to 175°C (350°F). Mix and grind the bell peppers and garlic together. Brown in oil till it gets soft then put it in a bowl and allow it to cool. Add spices, jalapenos, and the two kinds of cheese and mix thoroughly. Slice through the thinnest part of the chicken and open it like a book. Put a large cheese batter dollop inside it and close it with a toothpick, then add salt and pepper. Allow it to fry in either butter or oil before placing it in a baking dish. The leftover cheese batter should be put in the baking dish. You can then bake the big dollop of cheese batter inside the oven for about 15 minutes until you are sure the chicken breasts are thoroughly cooked. Don't forget to remove the inserted toothpick before you start serving. This special low carb recipe goes well with leafy greens and a moderate amount of guacamole or sour cream.

Oven-Baked Paprika Chicken with Rutabaga

Net carbohydrate content (in grams) – 15g

Estimated Preparation time- 40minutes

Ingredients:

i) Two chicken thighs (900g)
ii) Two rutabaga or root celery (900g)
iii) Four ounces of olive oil or butter (120g)
iv) One tablespoon of paprika powder salt and pepper
v) One cup of homemade mayonnaise (about 240ml)

Guidelines:

Heat up your oven to around 200°C (400°F). Separate the chicken quarters and position them in a baking dish. Remove the outer covering of the rutabaga and then cut it into two to three-inch pieces so that both rutabaga and chicken will get cooked at the same time.

Add salt and pepper while sprinkling chipotle on top of it. You should also add olive oil or butter and mix thoroughly. Then bake it in the oven for about 40mins until the chicken is completely cooked. If the rutabaga or chicken starts changing color toward the final stage of the baking, reduce the heat being applied. When serving, do so with a good amount of mayonnaise or whipped lemon butter. This is a very flavorful dish that replaces potatoes with rutabaga to keep the carbs low.

Cheese Chips

Estimated Preparation time- 10minutes

Ingredients:

i) 1/2 pound of sliced cheese like provolone, cheddar, etc. (225g)

ii) 1/2 teaspoon of paprika powder

Guidelines:

Heat up your oven to around 200°C (400°F). Position the sliced cheeses on a baking plate lined with parchment paper. Add a little paprika powder on top of and place it in the oven for ten minutes, depending on the level of thickness of the sliced cheeses. Be very careful so you don't burn the cheese slices when you are getting to the final stage of the cooking as burned cheese have a tendency of giving a bitter taste. Allow it to cool and enjoy with a drink or guacamole.

Low-Carb Banana Waffles

Estimated Preparation time- 10minutes

Ingredients:

- i) Two ripe bannas
- ii) Four big eggs
- iii) 3/4 cup of almond flour (200ml)
- iv) 3/4 cup of coconut milk (200ml)
- v) One tablespoon of psyllium husk powder
- vi) One teaspoon of baking powder powder

- vii) One pinch salt
- viii) 1/2 teaspoon of vanilla
- ix) One teaspoon of cinnamon
- x) Butter or coconut oil

Guidelines:

Mix all the ingredients together thoroughly and let it be for a while. Place the mixed ingredients in a frying pan and fry with coconut oil or butter. You may choose to serve with whipped coconut cream, melted butter, and fresh berries. This a good breakfast option with dairy-free waffles for people who can take a low-carb meal.

Low-Carb Pizza

Estimated Preparation time- 25 minutes

Ingredients:

- i) Six ounces of shredded cheese, provolone or mozzarella (175g)
- ii) Four eggs

iii) Four tablespoons of tomato paste
iv) One teaspoon of oregano
v) Two ounces of pepperoni
vi) Olives
vii) Another four ounces of shredded cheese

Guidelines:

Heat up your oven to around 200°C (400°F). Whisk the four eggs and blend them in six ounces of cheese. Spread the cheese together with the egg batter on a baking plate with parchment paper and make a rectangular pizza or two round circles if you prefer round pizzas. Leave it inside the oven for fifteen minutes until the pizza changes to golden color, then remove it and allow it to cool for a minute. Heat up your oven again to around 225°C (450°F). Place the tomato paste on the crust and add oregano, topping it up with four ounces of cheese while placing the pepperoni and olives on top. Leave it inside the oven for another five minutes until it turns golden brown in color. You can top it up with mushrooms, salami, blue cheese and salad, and then serve.

Low-Carb Tex-Mex Casserole

Estimated Preparation time- 20 minutes

Ingredients:

i) One and a half pounds of ground beef

ii) One and a half can of crushed tomatoes

iii) Two ounces of pickled jalapeños (56g)

iv) 200g of shredded cheese like Monterey Jack

v) One cup of sour cream (240ml)

vi) One handful of finely chopped chives or green onions

vii) Two tablespoons of olive oil or butter

viii) Homemade guacamole and taco seasoning

ix) Two teaspoons of chili powder and two teaspoons of paprika powder

x) One teaspoon of salt and one teaspoon of cumin powder

xi) One pinch of cayenne pepper

xii) Two teaspoons of onion or garlic powder

Guidelines:

Heat up your oven to around 200°C (400°F). Deep-fry the one and a half ground beef in butter, and add tomatoes and taco seasoning. Put the ground beef mix in a baking dish while placing cheese and jalapenos on top. Place on the upper rack of the oven for about 15 minutes, and then chop the chives smoothly and mix it with the sour cream. This goes well with guacamole, sour cream, and a green salad.

Soft Low-Carb Loaf of Bread

Estimated Preparation time- 40 minutes

Ingredients:

i)One cup of almond flour(250ml)

ii)3/4 cup of coconut flour (200ml)

iii)1/3 cup of sesame seeds(80ml)

iv)1/2 cup of flaxseeds (120ml)

v)1/4 cup of psyllium husk

vi)Three teaspoons of baking powder

vii)One teaspoon of caraway or fennel

viii)Six big eggs

ix)One teaspoon of salt

x)1/2 pound of cream cheese(220g)

xi)1/3 cup of melted butter or coconut oil

xii)3/4 cup of heavy whipping cream(200ml)

xiii) One tablespoon of poppy or sesame seeds

Guidelines:

Heat up your oven to around 175°C (350°F). Blend all dry ingredients together except poppy or sesame seeds that will be used later on to top it up. Whip the remaining ingredients together in a different bowl until the batter becomes smooth. Add the blended dry ingredients to the smoothened batter and mix thoroughly. Pour into a bread form parchment paper and bake if for about 45minutes. Pierce the bread with a knife to check if it's ready, then bring it out from the oven and remove the bread from the form while allowing it to cool on a rack. Slice the bread and store the remaining in the freezer. This is a very compact and satisfying low-carb bread option.

Blue-Cheese Dressing

Estimated Preparation time- 5 minutes

Ingredients:

    i)Five ounces of dry blue cheese(140g)

    ii)Six ounces of Greek yogurt

    iii)1/2 cup of homemade mayonnaise

    iv)Two tablespoons of finely chopped fresh parsley

    v)Salt and pepper

    vi)Water or heavy cream

This is a kind of low-carb cold dip sauce that is best taken with chicken, meat, on a salad or as a dip sauce.

Keto Garlic Bread

Estimated Preparation time- 40 minutes

Ingredients:

i) 1¼ cups of almond flour and two teaspoons of baking powder
ii) Five tablespoons of ground psyllium husk powder
iii) One teaspoon of sea salt
iv) Two teaspoons of white wine vinegar or apple cider vinegar
v) Three big white eggs and ½ tablespoon of garlic powder
vi) 1¼ cups boiling water (300 ml)
vii) Garlic butter and one minced small garlic clove
viii) Four ounces of 110g butter at room temperature

Guidelines:

Heat up your oven to around 175°C (350°F). Blend all the dry ingredients together in a bowl and add moderately hot water. Add the three white eggs and vinegar to the blended dry ingredients inside the bowl and whisk it with your hand for around 30seconds. Form into ten pieces hot dog buns with your moist hands but make sure you the dough are not over mixed. Bake on the lower rack of the oven for about 40 minutes and ensure there is enough space between them to increase their size without overlapping into each other during baking. Prepare the garlic butter while baking the bread and mix all the ingredients together and store inside the refrigerator. Take the buns out of the oven and allow it to cool. Spread the garlic butter on the buns after cutting them into different parts. Heat up your oven to around 225°C (425°F) and bake the garlic bread for around 10minutes until the color becomes golden brown. This low-carb bread goes well as an appetizer and as a snack as well.

Coconut Porridge

Estimated Preparation time- 10 minutes

Ingredients:

i)One ounce of butter (25g)

ii) One egg

iii) One tablespoon of coconut flour

iv) One pinch of psyllium seed husks

v) Four tablespoons of coconut cream

vi) A little salt

Sausage with Creamed Green Cabbage

Estimated Preparation time- 30 minutes

Ingredients:

i) 1½ pounds of great quality sausages (700g)
ii) Two tablespoons of butter for frying
iii) Two ounces of butter (60g)
iv) 1¼ cups of heavy whipping cream salt and pepper (300 ml)
v) ½ cup of fresh parsley (120 ml)
vi) Creamed Green Cabbage and ½ lemon

vii) 1½ pounds of finely chopped green cabbage, finely chopped (700 g)

Guidelines

Heat up your frying pan and cook the sausage by following the instructions written on the package. Fry the pan to melt it in another frying pan and add sauté and green cabbage, leave it for some minutes till it changes color to golden brown. Add the 1¼ cups of heavy whipping cream and allow it to simmer until the cream reduces. Add salt and pepper to give it a delicious taste and then serve with parsley and lemon zest. You can leave it as is or you can decide to serve it with salad.

Mushroom Omelet

Estimated Preparation time- 20 minutes

Ingredients:

i) Three eggs and 1/5 onion

ii) One ounce of butter for frying (25g) and one ounce of shredded cheese (25g)

iii) Two to three fresh mushrooms

iv) Salt and pepper

Guidelines:

Mix the three eggs in a bowl and add a pinch of salt and pepper. Whisk the eggs inside a batter with a fork and add salt and spices. Whisk the mashed eggs into a batter, preferably with a fork and add spices and salts. Melt the butter in a frying pan and pour it in the batter after the butter must have been melted. Sprinkle cheese, mushrooms, and onion as soon as the omelet begins to get firm when cooking, then ease around the edges of the omelet with the use of a spatula then bend it over in two halves. Remove the pan from the heat and place the omelet on a plate as soon as its color changes to golden brown. This delicious omelet goes well with a crispy salad.

Hamburger Patties with Creamy Tomato Sauce

Estimated Preparation time- 20 minutes

Ingredients:

i)1½ pounds of ground beef(700g)

ii)One big egg and one tablespoon of butter

iii)Three ounces of feta cheese(75g)

iv)One teaspoon of salt and one tablespoon of olive oil

v)Two ounces of finely chopped parsley(50g)

vi)One pinch of black pepper and tablespoon of tomato paste

vii)Salt and pepper

viii) Five fluid ounces of heavy whipping cream(150ml)

ix) Gravy

Guidelines:

Mix all the ingredients together and form eight oblong patties from the mixed ingredients. Fry the mixed ingredients with both butter and olive oil on a moderately heated hotplate until the patties change to an attractive color. Pour the whipping cream together with the tomato paste into the frying pan whenever you notice that the patties are almost done. Mix thoroughly and let the cream boil together with it. This can be served together with Parsley.

Cranberry Muffin Jubilee

Estimated Preparation time- 30 minutes

Net carbohydrate content (in grams) – 4.8g

Ingredients:

i) Twelve ounces of cream cheese

ii) Five soft eggs

iii) Fifteen packets of Splenda (sugar substitute)

iv) Two teaspoons of vanilla

v) 1 ½ cups of whole almond meal

vi) One cup of unprocessed wheat bran

vii) One teaspoon of baking powder

viii) One cup of whole or coarsely chopped cranberries (fresh or frozen)

Guidelines:

Heat up your oven to around 325°F. Grease the surface of a 12-cup muffin pan and pour the cream cheese and two eggs in the container of an electric mixer. Press hard until it becomes smooth and soft. Add the remaining eggs one after the other, pressing each of the added eggs briefly. Slowly stir the rest of the ingredients except the cranberries until you are certain the mixture has blended properly. Fill up the muffin pans to its brim and bake the muffins for about 20 minutes until the color turns golden brown. Freeze the muffins and thaw at room temperature.

Blueberry Muffin Jubilee

Estimated Preparation time- 30minutes

Net carbohydrate content (in grams) – 4.8g

Ingredients:

i) Twelve ounces of cream cheese

ii) Five soft eggs

iii) Fifteen packets of Splenda (sugar substitute)

iv) Two teaspoons of vanilla

v) 1 ½ cups of whole almond meal

vi) One cup of unprocessed wheat bran

vii) One teaspoon of baking powder

viii) One cup of whole blueberries (fresh or frozen)

ix) Two teaspoons of grated lemon peel

Guidelines:

Heat up your oven to around 325°F. Grease the surface of a 12-cup muffin pan and pour the cream cheese and two eggs in the container of an electric mixer. Press hard until it becomes smooth and soft. Add the remaining eggs one after the other, pressing each of the added eggs briefly. Slowly stir the rest of the ingredients except the grated lemon peel and blueberries until you are certain the mixture has blended properly. Fill up the muffin pans to its brim and bake the muffins for about 20 minutes until the color turns golden brown. Freeze the muffins and thaw at room temperature.

Protein Bread

Estimated Preparation time- 30 minutes

Ingredients:

i) 3/4 cup soy isolate

ii) Two tablespoons of white powdered egg

iii) Two packets of Splenda(sugar substitute)

iv) Two tablespoons of baking powder

v) Dash salt

vi) Five tablespoons of heavy cream

viii) Three big eggs
ix) Dash cream of tartar
x) 1/4 cup water
xi) 1/4 cup oil

Guidelines :

Heat up your oven to around 400°F and spray the pan. Mix the white powdered eggs with cream of tartar until stiff. In a separate container, mix the three big eggs yolks together with cream, water, and oil. Sieve in the dry ingredients and mix thoroughly with the aid of an electric mixer. Carefully roll the mixed ingredients inside the powdered egg whites. Place it in a pan and smoothen the utmost part slightly. Leave it inside the oven for twenty-five minutes or until bread is nicely browned.

Hot Flax Cereal

Estimated Preparation time- 5 minutes

Net carbohydrate content (in grams) – 6g

Ingredients:

i) 1/4 cup flax meal

ii) 1/4 cup light cream

iii) 1/3 cup water

iv) One packet of Splenda (sugar substitute)

v) Cinnamon

Guidelines:

Mix all the listed ingredients thoroughly and place in the microwave for just two minutes. This goes well as a breakfast for anybody on a low-carb diet plan.

Pineapple Syrup

Estimated Preparation time- 5 minutes

Ingredients:

i) 1/2 cup of water

ii) One teaspoon of pineapple extract

iii) 1/2 tablespoon of liquid Splenda

iv) 1/4 teaspoon of guar gum

Guidelines:

This is an-easy to prepare low-carb syrup. Add one teaspoon of pineapple extract and ½ tablespoon of liquid Splenda inside boiling water. Add guar gum and allow it to stick together for a couple of minutes. Then take as is.

Ham Sauce

Estimated Preparation time- 5 minutes

Net carbohydrate content (in grams) – 5.7g

Ingredients:

    i) One tablespoon of butter

    ii) One tablespoon of soy flour

    iii) 1/4 cup of light cream

    iv) 1/4 cup of water

    v) One teaspoon of Dijon mustard

    vi) Four ounces of chopped ham

Guidelines:

This delicious low-carb sauce could be served with two crepes each. Melt one tablespoon of butter and stir in soy flour. Add cream, Dijon mustard, and water, and mix thoroughly until the mixture becomes very thick. Add four ounces of chopped ham and mix.

Creamy Cheese Sauce

    Estimated Preparation time- 5 minutes

Net carbohydrate content (in grams) – 5.7g

Ingredients:

i) 1/4 cup of heavy cream

ii) Four ounces of grated cheddar

iii) Two ounces of cream cheese

iv) 1/4 teaspoon of paprika dash

v) Worcestershire sauce

Guidelines:

Moderately heat up a small pan and melt the heavy cream, cheddar, and cream cheese inside it. Add paprika and Worcestershire sauce and stir continuously until it melts.

Marinade

Estimated Preparation time- 5 minutes

Net carbohydrate content (in grams) – 5.7g

Ingredients:

    i) 1/8 cup of oil

    ii) 1/8 cup of soy sauce

    iii) 1/8 cup of balsamic vinegar

    iv) 4 "shots" Worcestershire garlic powder

    v) ginger

Guidelines:

Mix all the listed ingredients in a zip lock bag. Marinate a chicken or your preferred meat in a bag and keep in a refrigerator for 24hours. Rotate the bag intermittently.

Swiss & Crab Pie

    Estimated Preparation time- 5 minutes

Net carbohydrate content (in grams) – 5.7g

Ingredients:

i) One cup of shredded Swiss cheddar

ii) Eight ounces of crab meat

iii) Three beaten eggs

iv) 3/4 cup of heavy cream

v) 1/4 cup of water

vi) 1/2 teaspoon of salt

vii) Dry mustard to give it a delicious taste.

Guidelines

Heat up your oven up to around 325°F. Add the shredded cheddar inside a pie pan and spray lightly with PAM. Top it up with crab and then mix the remaining listed ingredients thoroughly before pouring it into the pie pan. Bake for about 40 minutes and you are done.

Can I Ask A Favor?

If you enjoyed this book, found it useful or otherwise then I'd appreciate it if you would post a short review on Amazon. I do read all the reviews personally so that I can continually write what people are wanting.

If you'd like to leave a review then, please visit the link below:

Thanks for your support!

www.ingramcontent.com/pod-product-compliance
Lightning Source LLC
Chambersburg PA
CBHW060406190526
45169CB00002B/780